Understanding the Faith

A Workbook for Communicants Classes
and Others Preparing to Make a Public Confession of Faith

REVISED EDITION

STEPHEN SMALLMAN

This workbook belongs to _____

P&R PUBLISHING

P.O. BOX 817 • PHILLIPSBURG • NEW JERSEY 08865-0817

Unless otherwise indicated, Scripture quotations are from *ESV Bible* ® (*The Holy Bible, English Standard Version* ®). Copyright © 2001 by Crossway Bibles, a publishing ministry of Good News Publishers. Used by permission. All rights reserved.

Graphics and design by Rev. Robert Smallman

The image appearing on page 1 (and throughout) is the property of the Church Art Works; the three images on pages 2–3 (and throughout), of ClickArt; and the image on page 34, of Art Explosion. All five images are used by permission of the owners.

Printed in the United States of America.

ISBN-13: 978-1-59638-186-5

Table of Contents

A Word to Teachers and Parents

From 1967 to 1996 I served as pastor of the McLean Presbyterian Church in McLean, Virginia. In my early years I searched for materials that would help me prepare the children of the congregation to understand the elements of the faith as part of their public profession of faith. This is what we Presbyterians usually call a Communicants Class. When nothing suitable was found, I began writing lessons myself and through the years I revised them again and again. I taught the class myself up until the time I moved away from that ministry. The privilege of working with those young people at such a critical moment in their lives (and partnering with parents who had laid the foundation) was one of the great joys of my ministry.

In 2001 my brother, Rev. Robert Smallman, helped me revise the materials into a much more appealing format and Presbyterian & Reformed Publishing made them available to a wider audience. I am very happy to say that since that time *Understanding the Faith* has been used by dozens of churches to prepare their young people to publicly confess their faith. But it has also become a resource for home-schooling parents and for people wanting a basic outline to introduce new believers to the essentials of the faith.

For the 2009 edition we have not made any significant changes in content, but we are making some changes in format you should be aware of:

1). The lessons will be formatted for use with the English Standard Version. The ESV is the preferred translation by an increasing number of churches that use *Understanding the Faith*. Those continuing to use the New International Version or other versions will still be able to answer most questions, but they should be aware that there will be occasional differences of wording.

2). The lessons will be formatted to conform to the classic edition of the Westminster Shorter Catechism. Copies of this older version are part of the public domain, and we believe the language is still accessible to modern users.

3). We are not including specific membership vows. This is still the focus of lesson 15, and if these lessons are being used for a public confession of faith you should be prepared to present and explain the vows of your particular denomination or church.

I am not providing a set of answers, because I think they should be self-evident as you study the Scriptures and the Shorter Catechism for yourself. When I taught the class (which consisted of reviewing the lesson by letting the students read their answers, and then discussing key points), I would make it very clear to the students that I expected them to come to class prepared — including the fact that the parents had signed the lesson. Very soon after the start of the class I would get in touch with the parents and encourage them to not just sign off on the lesson, but to actually review it after the young people had done their best to complete it. I had many, many expressions of gratitude from parents who appreciated what they had learned themselves as well as the opportunity it had provided to speak with their children about the truths of the faith.

One side benefit of the course is that by the end, the students not only can find their way through Scripture, but also do a good job of interpretation. In the early weeks, take extra time to help those who have not done much Scripture study to find their way in the Bible. If you use this in a church setting, it will be a challenge fitting this 18-week class into a church calendar. After several experiments, I settled on a class late Sunday afternoons from the first Sunday in December until late April. I have been told about many other creative ways that churches have incorporated *Understanding the Faith* into their overall Christian education ministry. However it is done, it is essential that we give our children this firm grounding in the faith.

It is best to begin each week with a review of key points from previous lessons. The catechism carefully develops a system of doctrine, and I have tried to follow that system. The students should see this logical progression of thought, so be sure to point out to them how one theme leads to the next. It is particularly important to spend several weeks reviewing the few things I assign the students to memorize: Question #4 ("What is God?"), the Lord's Prayer, and the Ten Commandments.

You will note that in lessons 10–13 I am asking the students to consider their own relationship to Christ. In my own teaching experience it was at this stage that I sought out a time to speak with them personally about this issue before I brought them to meet with the elders for the membership interview. In some cases the young people were not ready to make a personal confession, and in such cases we waited until they were. It is important that we respect each student's sensitivities, and not make assumptions about the young people's faith just because they complete the course.

I pray that these lessons will be helpful to you and the students you teach. I welcome any comments or questions. You are also welcome to visit the website of Birthline Ministries where I describe the other materials I have written for parents and new believers.

Stephen Smallman

steve@birthlineministries.com
www.birthlineministries.com

THE MEANING OF CHURCH MEMBERSHIP

This is the first of 17 lessons that you will be completing as a member of the Communicants Class. After you complete each lesson, check it with your parent(s) and have one sign it. It should be brought to class the next week.

Find answers to the questions by looking in the paragraphs above them or by looking in the Bible (English Standard Version — ESV) or the Westminster Shorter Catechism (S.C.). **You do not need to guess** unless the question asks what you think about something.

Please write down any questions you have and bring them to class. Questions are always welcome!

1. What was the reason for God's creating man? (See Shorter Catechism #1) Man's chief end is to

    _____

    and _____ .

    a. **To glorify God** means to give him the place of honor; it is like shining a light on something to show how beautiful it is.

        Look up these verses and write down ways we can honor or glorify God:

        Psalm 50:23; 86:12 _____

        John 4:23 _____

        Matthew 5:16 _____

        I Corinthians 10:31 _____

    b. **To enjoy God** means that human beings are happiest and most satisfied when they know God.

        Augustine was a great Christian who lived around A.D. 400. He said to God: *"Thou hast made us for thyself and our hearts are restless until they rest in thee."*

Rewrite that saying in modern English the way you understand it: _____

_____

_____

Think about it

In the beginning, God created the universe, the earth, and everything on the earth, including man. He made it all good, and man could enjoy God's good creation and enjoy being with God. But man chose to disobey God and to live without him. This is sin, and sin has brought death, and sickness, and hatred and evil into God's world. But God refused to let sin ruin his world and had a plan to overcome sin. This plan was that he would rescue many, many people from sin and make them his special people, his family.

2. The Bible says man chose to disobey God and live without him. (Find the answer in the paragraphs above.)

   a. What is this choice called? _____

   b. What has sin brought into God's good world? _____

   _____

   _____

   c. Will God allow sin and death to ruin his creation?

   _____

3. What is God's plan? _____

   _____

   _____

4. What is the Church?

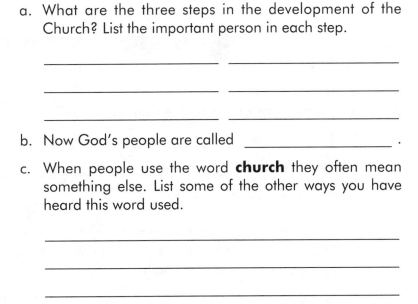

One name for this people or family is the <u>Church</u>. The Church is a gathering of people who trust and serve the true God. God has always had his Church: at first the family of Abraham was the Church; later God used Moses to lead the Hebrew nation out of Egypt and the Hebrews (Israel) became his Church. Finally Jesus came and taught that all who truly believed in him could be part of his Church. So the Church was first a family, then a nation, then gatherings of people from all nations. Now God's special people are called Christians.

Think about it

a. What are the three steps in the development of the Church? List the important person in each step.

_____ _____

_____ _____

_____ _____

b. Now God's people are called _____ .

c. When people use the word **church** they often mean something else. List some of the other ways you have heard this word used.

_____

_____

_____

_____

What do YOU think?

Think about it

Today the Church is called the Body of Christ. That means Jesus is the head, and we are the parts of the body. Jesus told the people in his Church always to remind themselves that this is true by having Communion (also called the Lord's Supper, because it is just like Jesus' last supper with the disciples). Communion is a way of showing that we have taken Jesus into our lives and are part of his Church. The name <u>Communicants Class</u> comes from the word <u>communion</u>. The Communicants Class is to help you prepare to become a communicant member of one gathering of Jesus' Church. If you were baptized as an infant or a child, you were received as a non-communing member of the church. Now that you are old enough to understand much more about Jesus, you need to study so that you can confess him as your own Lord and be a communicant member.

5.   What is one term we use for the Church today?

_____

a. Who is the head? _____

Who are the parts of the Body?_____

_____

b. What is the ceremony Jesus gave us to remind ourselves that he is our source of strength?

_____

also called the _____

c. What does taking Communion show? _____

_____

_____

6. Were you baptized as a child?_____

   a. Ask your parents why they had you baptized and write a summary of their answer.

   _____

   _____

   _____

   _____

   b. If you were not baptized, ask your parents why they decided not to do that. Summarize their answer.

   _____

   _____

   _____

   _____

7. Do you want to be part of Jesus' Church?_____

8. What is the name of the particular gathering of Jesus' church which you attend?

   _____

Don't Forget!

Date Completed _____

Parent's Initials_____

THE SCRIPTURES

I. The Importance of the Bible

1. People have always asked very serious questions about life: How did everything begin? Is there a God? What is he like? Can I know God? Is there life after death? How can my sins be forgiven? These are very important questions, and people have had many different answers. How can we know who is right when many of the answers are very different and cannot all be true?

    a. What are some different ideas people have about God? _____

    _____

    _____

    b. What are some explanations you have heard for the beginning of the universe? _____

    _____

    _____

2. The Bible came by "revelation."

Think of the right answers being behind a heavy curtain. We can guess what is behind the curtain, but we don't know for sure. The best thing would be to pull it back and see what is there. The Bible does just that — God pulls back the curtain to tell us what he is like and what life is all about. The word for this is <u>revelation</u>. So to understand God and life and death, we do not guess and hope we are right. We study what God has said.

Think about it

a. Use the idea of a curtain to define revelation. _____

_____

_____

b. Without God's revealing himself to us, the best we can do is _____ about the meaning of life.

3. Look up Deuteronomy 29:29 and answer these questions:

a. Has God told us everything about himself? _____

b. Do you think we could understand if he did? _____

c. Should we be surprised if we come to questions about God we cannot answer? _____

d. Why has God revealed the things that he has? _____

_____

_____

4. God has revealed himself in ways other than just through the Bible, but we need the Bible to tell us these other ways. From these verses tell how God is revealed:

a. Romans 1:20 _____

b. Romans 2:15 _____

c. Hebrews 1:1_____

5. But the only rule from God to actually direct us how we may glorify and enjoy him is: (S.C. #2) _____

_____

a. Look up Deuteronomy 31:24–26. Moses was an old man ready to die. But before he died, what did he do with the words of the Law? He finished _____ them in a _____. Then the book of the law (the Bible) was put by the side of the _____ of the covenant to remain as a _____ against them. (v. 26)

b. Look up Matthew 5:17, 18. How important did Jesus say the Bible was? _____

_____

_____

There are many today who ignore the Bible or who try to say that it is no different from any other religious book. But those who follow Jesus Christ love the Bible because Jesus did. They try to understand the Bible and believe what it says because that is what Jesus taught us to do.

Think about it

6. Why do those who follow Jesus Christ love the Bible?

_____

_____

II. The Teaching of the Bible

1. The Bible records very interesting and accurate history. It sometimes mentions scientific matters. It has beautiful poetry, but two basic teachings are found in the Bible that are more important than anything else. What are they? (Look up S.C. #3)

    What _____

    and what _____

2. Look up II Timothy 3:14–17 and answer these questions:

    a. How long had Timothy known the teaching of the Bible? (v. 15) _____

    b. What did he learn from the Bible? (v. 15) _____

    _____

    c. How much of the Scripture is inspired by God (God-breathed)? (v. 16) _____

    d. What is something else that happened when God breathed out? (Genesis 1:3) _____

    _____

e. What are four uses for the Bible (Scripture)? (v. 16)

1) _____

2) _____

3) _____

4) _____

f. What does the Bible do for the Christian ("man of God")
who understands it? (v. 17) _____

_____

_____

3. The Bible came from God.

Think about it

The Bible itself teaches that it is not an ordinary book. It is a creation of God. We have it because God spoke. In creation God spoke, and the world came into being. The Bible is a different kind of creation because God spoke to men and then made sure they wrote exactly what he wanted them to write. But it is still his creation, not man's.

Look up II Peter 1:20, 21.

a. When Peter speaks of prophecy here he says (v. 20), "no prophecy of_____." So he is talking about the Bible.

b. This prophecy (Scripture) did not come from _____
_____ .(v. 21)

c. But men spoke from _____ as they were _____ by the _____
_____. (v. 21)

4. The Bible is not so much one book but a library of 66 books written by about 36 different people between 1400 B.C. and A.D. 100.

a. How many books are in the Bible?_____

How many in the Old Testament? _____

How many in the New Testament? _____

b. What is the main difference between the Old and New Testaments? _____

_____

c. How many different people did God inspire to write the books of the Bible? _____

d. Put these periods of Bible history in the proper order by using the numbers 1–8:

_____ Jesus came into the world, died on the cross, and rose again.

_____ God called Abraham to be the father of a great nation and promised him a son.

_____ David was the greatest King of Israel; his son Solomon built the Temple.

_____ God created the world and made man and woman in his own image.

_____ Peter and Paul and others went everywhere preaching about Jesus.

_____ God punished his people and sent them to Babylon for 70 years.

_____ Moses led Israel out of Egypt and through 40 years in the desert.

_____ Jesus went back to Heaven and sent the Holy Spirit to fill his disciples.

What do
YOU think?

Date Completed _____

Parent's Initials_____

Lesson 3

GOD–WHAT IS HE LIKE?

1. According to S.C. #3, what is the **first** principal thing taught in the Scriptures? _____

    _____

2. What is God? (Look up S.C. #4.)

    "God is a _____,

    _____, _____,

    and _____, in his _____,

    _____, _____,

    _____, _____,

    _____, and _____."

    a. Many have said this is the finest brief definition of God to be found.

        Memorize this answer to S.C. #4.

    b. Define these adjectives: *infinite, eternal, unchangeable* (use a dictionary if necessary).

        Infinite _____

        Eternal_____

        Unchangeable _____

3. What does John 4:24 tell us about God? _____

    _____

    a. God is an infinite spirit. This means there are no physical limits on God. Look up the second commandment (Exodus 20:4) and write why you think it is so important not to make images of God.

        _____

        _____

        _____

b. God is personal.

Think about it

Some say that if God is spirit then he is only a force or a power with no personality (he cannot think or talk or listen or plan). But we do not need a body to be a person (we live after our bodies die), and without a body God is an infinite and personal spirit. Look up these verses and write down what God can do because he is a person rather than just a force.

Psalm 55:16, 17 _____

_____

Psalm 103:8, 13 _____

_____

Proverbs 3:19, 20 _____

_____

Proverbs 15:3 _____

_____

John 3:16 _____

_____

4. Look up Psalm 90:2.

a. Which of the three adjectives (infinite, eternal, unchangeable) does this verse especially speak about?

_____

b. Little children often ask, "Who made God?" or, "When did God begin?" How would you answer these questions?

_____

_____

_____

5. Look up Malachi 3:6. Which of the three adjectives does this verse describe? _____

Of course, just like a mother who loves a child whether she is cuddling or spanking him, God changes the way he acts toward us (in the Bible this is how God "repents") without ever changing his Being.

Think about it

6. Sometimes, to describe God the prefix "omni" is used; it means **all**. So the word omni**present** means God can be everywhere at the same time. Omni**potent** means God is all powerful; there is no limit to what he can do. Omni**scient** means all knowing; God knows everything that can be known — past, present, and future. Look up these verses and tell which of the "omni" words is described.

Psalm 139:1–6 _____

Psalm 139:7–12 _____

Psalm 135:5–7 _____

7. Look up I Timothy 1:17. Then write a brief prayer telling God how you feel about his greatness.

_____

_____

_____

_____

_____

_____

Date Completed _____

Parent's Initials_____

God, the Three in One

I. There is only one God.

Since you have been through several years of school, you know that one of the basic ideas of teaching is to start with simple ideas. After they are learned, you move on to harder ones. Some of you have made fun of younger brothers or sisters because they were trying hard to understand something you thought was easy. You forgot that the same idea was hard for you once. God teaches us in the Bible the same way. Before he revealed that he is one God in three persons, he made sure we understood the simpler idea that he is one. When people try to guess what is behind the curtain (remember, in the Bible God pulls back the curtain —that is revelation), they come up with the idea that there are many different gods. That is a false idea and, in the Old Testament especially, God again and again teaches that he is the only god there is. People today don't often have many gods, but they do have things that are more important than God; and that makes those things gods.

1. Answer these questions from the paragraph above.

    a. A good way to teach is to first teach the _____ then the_____ .

b. Before God could teach us he is three in one, he had to teach us he is _____ .

c. When people try to guess what God is like, what idea do they often have? _____

_____

d. What does question #5 of the S.C. teach?

_____

e. Do people have false gods today? _____
Can you think of some?

_____

_____

2. God has a special name for himself.

Think about it

In the Old Testament one way God revealed himself was by the different names he used for himself. For example, as the Creator or the Ruler of nations, the Bible uses just the word God. But when God comes to those he especially loves, he has a special name — Jehovah (some write it Yahweh). Just as most people know you by one name but within your family you have a special name, so Jehovah is the special name used by those who know him. (Note: In most Bibles instead of the word Jehovah appearing, it is translated as LORD in small capital letters. When it is Lord in normal print, that is another word for God which means Master.)

a. Look up these verses and write in the name used for God.

Genesis 1:1,3 _____

Exodus 3:15, 16 _____

Psalm 8:1 _____ and _____

Jeremiah 50:34 _____

Matthew 6:9 _____

II. God is a trinity.

Once God had taught us that he is one (unity), he went on in the Bible, especially in the New Testament, to teach us that within his unity he is actually three persons. To express this we use the term tri-unity or <u>Trinity</u>. Often you will see references to the <u>Triune God</u>. In each case the word used shows that there is one God (not three) in three persons. These persons of the Trinity are God the Father, God the Son, and God the Holy Spirit.

Think about it

1. Look up S.C. #6. It says the Father, Son, and Holy Ghost (or Holy Spirit) are the same in _____. That means they are equally God and, therefore, are equal in _____ and _____.

   No person of the Trinity is more important or more wonderful than the other.

2. Because they cannot understand how God can be one and yet three, many people have said this is not true. They are usually _____nitarians, whereas Christians are _____nitarians.

3. No one can really understand how God can be three in one, but we believe it because that is what the Bible teaches.

   a. Look up John 1:1–5.

      1) What other book of the Bible starts, "In the beginning"? _____

      2) Does John say the Word was created? _____

      3) The Word was _____ .

4) Look at John 1:14. What does it say the Word did?

_____

and _____

Who is this talking about? _____

From before creation he has always been God the Son, even though he had an earthly birth. The same is true of God the Holy Spirit.

b. Did the Holy Spirit take part in creation? (Look up Genesis 1:2) _____

c. Look up John 14:15–17. In these verses God the

_____ is praying to God the _____

about the coming of God the _____ .

d. Look up Matthew 28:19. When people became followers of Jesus (disciples), they were to be baptized in the name of …

God the _____ ,

_____ , and

_____ .

Thus you can see that even though the word **Trinity** is not found in the Bible, it is a perfect word to use about God. He is one and yet three.

III. Prayer

Think about it

Even though God is *so* high above us, he still wants us to talk to him. When we talk to God, it is called prayer. Jesus (God the Son) gave us a prayer to help us learn how to talk to God our Father. It is called the "Lord's Prayer." There are five parts to the Lord's Prayer, and each part teaches us a different thing to pray about.

1. What is prayer? _____

   _____

2. What did Jesus give us to help us learn how to pray?

   _____

3. Because of Jesus' teaching, how can we now speak to God?

   "Our _____ who art _____." (God was never addressed this way in the Bible until Jesus came to show us the way to God.)

4. How many parts are there to the Lord's Prayer? _____

You can remember the Lord's Prayer by looking at your hand. The palm of the hand is the privilege we have to call God "Our Father," and the five fingers are the five different things we pray about when we talk to our Father.

Memorize the Lord's Prayer

   "Our Father, who art in heaven …

   ❶ *"hallowed be Thy Name …*

   ❷ *"Thy Kingdom come, thy will be done on earth as it is in heaven …*

   ❸ *"Give us this day our daily bread …*

   ❹ *"And forgive us our debts as we forgive our debtors …*

   ❺ *"And lead us not into temptation, but deliver us from evil …*

   "For thine is the Kingdom, and the power, and the Glory, forever. Amen."

   (These words were not from the prayer Jesus gave us, but Christians added them soon after Jesus lived, and now they are a part of the Lord's Prayer.)

This is what the five parts of the Lord's Prayer teach us.

   ❶ We worship and adore God, whom we can now call Father.

   ❷ We pray for God's rule in our hearts and all over the world.

   ❸ We pray for our daily needs.

❹ We ask for our sin to be forgiven and that we forgive others in the same way.

❺ We pray for God to guide and protect us.

5. Draw lines to match the words of the Lord's Prayer with what they teach.

"Hallowed be thy Name"   Prayer for God to protect and guide

"Thy Kingdom Come"   Prayer for our needs

"Give us this day"   Worship and Adoration

"Forgive us our debts"   Prayer for God's rule

"Lead us not"   Prayer for sin to be forgiven

Date Completed _____

Parent's Initials_____

GOD'S DECREES AND THEIR EXECUTION

Although the Triune God has always existed (God is eternal), there came a point in time when everything else that exists had a beginning. God created all things (Creation). But the Bible teaches that before God created he planned everything; and the creation and everything that has happened since creation is the carrying out of God's plan. The word used for this plan is decree. If you think of God's creation as a house, think of his decree as the blueprint or plan for the house. And once you build the house, you take care of it. When God takes care of his creation, the word used is providence.

1. Use the terms **decree**, **creation**, and **providence** in the proper way to describe how God works.

   The plan for a house is the _____ ;

   actually building the house is _____ ;

   taking care of it after building is _____ .

Everything God made (_____)

and how he guides his creation (_____)

follows exactly his eternal plan (_____).

Look up S.C. #8.

God executeth his _____ in the _____ of

_____ and _____ .

2. Look at S.C. #7.

a. How old is God's plan? _____

b. *"According to the counsel of his will"* means God made
    up his own mind what to do.

    Look up Isaiah 46:8–10.

    1) Who declares the end from the beginning? _____

    2) God's plan does not change. His counsel shall

        _____ .

    3) How much of God's purpose will be accomplished?

        _____

c. How much has God planned ("foreordained")? _____

    _____

d. Why has God planned everything? "for_____

    _____ ."

    1) Did God need to create the universe? _____

    2) Did God need to create man? _____

    3) Why then does man exist? (S.C. #1) _____

        _____

        _____

**What do
you think?**

3. God's plan includes our choices.

God's decrees include everything. Some people have said this makes people like puppets. They don't really think and choose; they have to do what God planned. But we are not puppets. In a marvelous way we cannot understand, God's plan includes our choices. So we make our own choices (many times bad choices), but at the same time we fulfill the plan of God. Consider these examples from the Bible:

Think about it

a. Look up Acts 2:23.

   1) Why was Jesus allowed to die? _____

   _____

   2) Who put him on the cross? _____

   _____

   3) Did these men do it because they had to since it was God's plan, or because they hated Jesus?

   _____

b. Were Adam and Eve forced to disobey God, or did they choose to disobey? _____

   Yet their choice to disobey was part of his plan, and he had already planned to deliver many, many people from sin.

c. Look up Ephesians 1:4. When had God chosen those Christians? _____

d. Nebuchadnezzar was a great conqueror of ancient Babylon. Nebuchadnezzar thought his own power made him great, but God took away his power.

   Look up Daniel 4:34, 35.

   1) Compared to God, what are the inhabitants of the earth? _____

2) Where are two places God's plan (will) is done?

"He does according to his will among _____

_____

and _____ *."*

3) Who can stop him (*"stay his hand"*)?

_____

e. How does it make you feel to know God has a plan that includes everything and that his plan will be carried out? _____

_____

_____

4. God carries out his plan through creation.
Look up S.C. #9.

a. With what did God make everything? _____

_____

b. According to Genesis 1:3, 6, 9, what did God have to do to create something from nothing?

_____

The catechism says he did it *"by* _____

_____ *."*

c. According to Genesis 1:31, what did God think about his creation? _____

_____

What do YOU think?

d. How God created the world.

We do not know exactly how God created his world or exactly how long it took. Some think the six "days" of Genesis 1 represent six long periods. Others think it only took six 24-hour days. The important fact is that God created the world — it didn't just happen. People who do not believe in God have tried in different ways to explain how the world got here. Sometimes they have tried to make others think their ideas were more scientific than believing in creation. But this is not so. One who believes in God loves science because it is a study of God's world.

Think about it

Explain why science and the Bible can go together.

_____

_____

_____

What is one question you have about science and the Bible?

_____

_____

_____

What do YOU think?

5. Look up these verses and list what God has created.

a. Genesis 1:3 _____

b. Genesis 1:26, 27 _____

c. Psalm 102:25 _____

d. Isaiah 40:26 _____

e. Hebrews 1:13, 14 _____

6. What was that final creation of God? (Genesis 1:26, 27)

_____

a. Who were the man and woman like? (Genesis 1:26)

_____

b. Look up S.C. #10.

List the ways man and woman were in God's image:

"... in _____ , _____ ,

and _____ with _____

over the other creatures."

c. What did God tell man and woman to do? (Genesis
1:28) _____

_____

_____

Just as God ruled over the entire creation, including
humans and angels, so human beings were to rule
over one portion of his creation — the earth. Some
day we will answer to God for how well we did the job
he gave us.

d. You are a creation of God and no one else is just like you.
List two things you like about the way God created you.

_____

_____

e. Write down one strength or gift or talent he has given you.

_____

What do
YOU think?

Date Completed _____

Parent's Initials_____

Don't forget!

Lesson 6

SIN

1. Providence, we have learned, is God's caring for his creation.

    Look up S.C. #11. It says God's works of providence are his

    most _____, _____ ,

    and _____ _____ and

    _____ everything in creation.
    Nothing is unimportant to God. Jesus taught that his Father even cares for the birds. (Matthew 6:26)

    But the **question** in S.C. #12 asks what _____ act of providence God exercised toward man. God has a special relationship to human beings who were created in his image.

    a. Look up and read Genesis 2:8–17.

        1) Where did God put the man and woman? (2:8, 15) _____

        _____

        2) What could they eat? (Genesis 2:16) _____

        _____

        3) Name the two special trees. (2:9) _____ ,

        and the tree of the _____

        of _____

        4) Why do you think they were special? _____

        _____

        5) What do you think was the reason for the command of 2:17? _____

        _____

        6) What was the penalty for disobedience? (2:17).

        _____

What do
YOU think?

b. S.C. #12 teaches that the command not to eat was part of a covenant of _____ .

Adam and Eve could have earned eternal life by perfect

_____ .

2. Angels and Satan

Think about it

> Into the perfect scene — a garden where a man and his wife enjoyed each other and God — came an intruder, Satan. One part of God's creation we do not know much about is the spiritual beings he made. These beings are often called angels, but we do not know how many angels there are or everything they do. It does seem that a large number rebelled against God and were cast out of heaven.

a. Look up Matthew 25:41, II Peter 2:4, and Jude 6, and tell what the future of these angels will be.

_____

b. The leader of these rebel angels has the name Devil or Satan, and he now lives on the earth, still trying to defeat God. He was either the serpent of Genesis 3:1, or he filled the serpent and spoke through it. What is Satan still trying to do? _____

_____

c. Look up and read Genesis 3:1–13.

1) Did the serpent (Satan) tell the woman to disobey God at first? (v. 1) _____

Instead he tried to get the woman to think of herself first and ignore what God wanted. What would the fruit do for Eve? (v. 5) _____

_____

2) Look at v. 4; then look up John 8:44. Jesus said Satan was the father of _____ .

Is Genesis 3:4 true or a lie? _____

3) Why did Adam and Eve hide? (v. 7)_____

_____

4) Why did God ask the questions of v. 11? _____

_____

_____

d. What is a one-word answer to S.C. #13?_____

e. What is sin? (Answer with S.C. #14.)_____

_____

_____

_____

1) What God says (his law) is what is right. *"Want of conformity"* means not living up to God's law, and *"transgression"* means actually breaking it. For example, God says we are to love him with all of our hearts. One person just ignores God, and another laughs at God and uses his name in vain.

Which of these examples is *"want of conformity"*?

_____

And which is *"transgression"*? _____

_____

Which is sin against God? _____

2) Doing wrong is sin, but what does James 4:17 say is also sin? _____

_____

_____

3) Look up James 1:13–15. According to this, check the right one to blame whenever we sin.

❑ God

❑ Satan

❑ Ourselves and what we want

❑ Other people — parents, teachers, etc.

4) Who is to blame for the sin of Adam and Eve?

_____

5) Who will answer to God for the sin you have
done? _____

3. Adam and Eve

**Think
about it**

It is important to understand that the Bible teaches that Adam and Eve were real people. We do not know all the details of other early humans (such as the cave men), but even scientists generally agree that all humans come from a single beginning. The Bible teaches that we are united with all humans of all ages by not only being of the same blood and DNA but also because the sin of Adam and Eve has affected us all. Adam acted for us all when he chose to disobey God, and we show that we agree with his choice when we constantly choose to do the same.

a. What is a one-word answer for S.C. #16? _____

b. What two things came to man because of the fall? (S.C. #17) *"the estate of* _____

and _____ *."*

1) Look at S.C. #18. This says that from Adam we are not only under his curse, but we now have original sin — something he did not have at creation.

Original sin has three parts:

✓ Guilt ...

God said disobeying him by eating the fruit would bring death.

Romans 6:23 says the wages of sin is _____ ,

and I Corinthians 15:22 says that in Adam all

_____.

So the *"guilt of Adam's first sin"* means we are all under the sentence of death.

✓ **Want (meaning we don't have) ...**

We are not born righteous or innocent — we grow up choosing to sin — it is our nature to sin. According to Ephesians 2:3, what are we *"by nature"*? _____

_____

✓ **Corruption ...**

This does not mean we are as corrupt or evil as we could be, but it does mean that every part of us and everything we do is guided by our sinful nature. According to Romans 3:10–12, how many are seeking after God and really doing good?

_____

2) All human misery, suffering, and poverty are a result of man's sin. But S.C. #19 speaks especially of what sin does to a person's relationship to God.

All mankind by their fall lost _____

with _____, are under his _____

and _____, and so made liable to...

_____ ,

_____ ,

_____ .

4. Without God we die.

Think about it

For man to be away from God is like a fish out of water. As a fish dies without water, so man dies without God. He is dead <u>spiritually</u> as he tries to live without God. He dies <u>physically</u> when the body stops working. And he dies <u>eternally</u> when he lives forever apart from God. Which of the three kinds of death are described in the following verses (they could refer to more than one)?

a) Ecclesiastes 3:19, 20 _____

b) John 11:14 _____

c) Romans 5:12 _____

d) Romans 6:23 _____

e) I Corinthians 15:22 _____

f) Revelation 21:8 _____

5. Sin will bring death to **you** some day (unless Jesus returns first). Are you afraid to die?

Explain briefly. _____

_____

_____

_____

_____

What do you think?

Date Completed _____

Parent's Initials_____

THE LAW OF GOD

1. According to S.C. #3, what is the **second** main thing the Bible teaches? _____

    a. What is the duty which God requireth of man? (S.C. #39)

    _____

    b. What did God at first reveal to man for the rule of his obedience? (S.C. #40) _____

    _____

    c. Where is the moral law summarized ("summarily comprehended")? (S.C. #41) _____

    _____

    d. What one word is the sum of the ten commandments? (S.C. #42) _____

    We are to love _____ and _____ .

2. The moral law

    Whenever someone tells us that we must obey, we must also, of course, be told what to obey. In the case of obedience to God, what we are to obey is called the **moral law**.

    a. The moral law is most clearly explained in the _____

    _____ .

    b. But there was moral law long before the commandments were given. In the Garden the moral law was the commandment not to eat of the tree. That told Adam what God expected from him.

    Look up Romans 2:15 and write how one knows the moral law without the ten commandments. _____

    _____

    Adam's conscience was perfect, but since the Fall even our conscience does not tell us the law in a perfect way.

Do you think "Let your conscience be your guide" is good advice? _____ Explain briefly. _____

_____

_____

Since our conscience is so weak, God spoke directly to his people and then wrote the law on stone. Look up Exodus 19 and 20 which tell of God's giving the commandments.

c. To whom did God give the Ten Commandments? (19:1–2) _____

They had gone out of _____ and came into

the wilderness of _____. There they encamped

before the _____ .

d. The Bible says God actually spoke to Israel.

What covered the mountain? (19:18) _____

What sound came before God spoke? (19:19) _____

_____

How did the people feel? (20:18)_____

_____

Did they need to feel that way? (20:20)_____

Why did God want them to see his power and majesty? (20:20) _____

_____

e. What did God say to introduce the commandments? (20:2 and S.C. #43) _____

_____

_____

(This is often called "The Preface.")

1) What name did he use for himself? (20:2) _____

_____

Why is that important? _____

_____

2) In the preface God told his chosen people that he loved them and had taken care of them. And because he loved them so much, he gave them his law. **This is important**. Many try to say that law and love are opposites and that love is more important than law.

    a)   Look up Matthew 5:19. Did Jesus believe love is more important than law? _____

    b)   According to Deuteronomy 10:13, why did God give the law? _____

        _____

f.   The commandments are in Exodus 20:3–17. Be sure to memorize them (in the short form listed on page 35, not the entire passage) and learn them in order since that is very important.

The first four are about our relationship to God and are summarized in Deuteronomy 6:5: _____

_____

_____

Since God wrote the commandments on two tables (flat pieces) of stone, this is called the **"first table"** of the law.

The **"second table"** contains the last six commandments and deals with our relationship to our neighbor. These are summarized by Leviticus 19:18:_____

_____

_____

THE TEN COMMANDMENTS

3. **Memorize** the Ten Commandments that are in the bold type below. Make sure to include the words of the Preface. (You'll understand later what the lines before each command are for.)

The PREFACE:

I am the LORD your God, who brought you out of the land of Egypt, out of the house of slavery.

THEREFORE:

First Table of the Law (How to love _____)

_____ 1. You shall have no other gods before me.

_____ 2. You shall not make for yourself a carved image.

_____ 3. You shall not take the name of the LORD your God in vain.

_____ 4. Remember the Sabbath day, to keep it holy.

Second Table of the Law (How to love your _____)

_____ 5. Honor your father and your mother.

_____ 6. You shall not murder.

_____ 7. You shall not commit adultery.

_____ 8. You shall not steal.

_____ 9. You shall not bear false witness.

_____ 10. You shall not covet.

---

4. Look at the questions of S.C. #46, 47, 50, 51, 54, 55. This is the same for all ten. First, the question asks what is _____ in the commandment

(what we should do), then the next question asks what is _____ in the commandment (what we should not do). This shows that the commandments are more than just rules, but they teach us something about life and about God.

Go back to the list of commandments. In the space before each commandment list these words that identify the principle behind each commandment: **Religion** (in front of the first commandment), **Worship** (in front of the second commandment), **Reverence**, **Rest**, **Authority**, **Life**, **Marriage**, **Property**, **Truth**, **Heart**.

a. Jesus taught us that we must follow the commandments in what we think and feel as well as in what we do. In Matthew 5:21, 22 how can we break the sixth commandment? _____

_____

Each of the other commandments can be understood in the same way.

b. Jesus also taught that all the duty God requires of us comes down to _____ .
(Matthew 22:37-39)

Did Jesus originate this teaching? _____

5. The law shows us who we are.

God's law is good. It was given to show us God's perfect standard. God is holy, and we are to be holy too. The law also explains God's way to live life (families are very important; we should work hard and tell the truth, etc.). But the law has another important purpose. When we think we are good enough to earn or deserve God's blessing, the law shows us we are sinners.

Think about it

a. Is it possible for anyone to keep the commandments of God perfectly? (Answer with S.C. #82) _____

Since the _____ no ordinary person can perfectly keep the commandments, but every day we break them in _____

_____ .

b. What does every sin deserve? (S.C. #84) _____

_____

_____

_____

6.   The Law of God is good, but it cannot bring forgiveness of sin or salvation. That takes the Gospel (**Law** is what we do for God; **Gospel** is what God does for us). According to Romans 8:3, what has God done that the law could not do? _____

_____

_____

So now we need to study the Gospel of Jesus Christ.

Date Completed _____

Parent's Initials _____

JESUS CHRIST—
THE COVENANT OF
GRACE; REDEMPTION

We are all sinners. Not only because we inherit a sinful nature from Adam, but because we ourselves choose to disobey God and his law. According to Romans 6:23, what is the payment we will receive for sin? _____

Look back to Lesson 6, page 31, and list the three kinds of death: _____

This is very different from the way God began his creation. It was all very good, and man and God walked together. In one word, yes or no, answer Question #20 of the S.C. Did God leave all mankind to perish in the estate of sin and misery? _____

The simple answer to #20 is "no." God is not going to allow Satan or man to ruin his wonderful creation. S.C. #20 also begins to explain God's plan to destroy sin.

1. Look first at the phrase "covenant of grace." A covenant is an agreement or contract that God makes with man. (People make covenants, too — like marriage.)

    a. According to S.C. #12, God first entered into a covenant of _____ with man, upon condition of perfect _____ .

    b. Did Adam and Eve keep that covenant? (S.C. #13)

        _____

    c. So God made a second covenant with man, a covenant of _____

        (S.C. #20). Since man can no longer obey, God chose to give man salvation as a gift.

2. Redemption, Redeemer, Ransom

Think about it

Notice the phrases: "Deliver them out of the estate of sin and misery" and "bring them into an estate of salvation." That describes one of the most important words in the Bible — REDEMPTION. You must understand this word. Redemption means rescue or deliverance through the payment of a price. The one who pays the price is the Redeemer. A person who has been delivered has been redeemed. The price paid for redemption is often called the ransom.

a. Define redemption. _____

_____

b. In these paragraphs fill in the blanks with one of the four underlined words.

1) If someone were kidnapped, to rescue or redeem him you would have to pay a _____ .

2) The redemption of a slave:

John was a slave, but he had a rich friend who offered to buy his freedom. This friend was John's _____ _____ and after he paid

the redemption price, _____ , John was redeemed.

3) The redemption of Israel:

God's people Israel were slaves in Egypt. But God loved them and rescued them from slavery. God is the _____

of Israel. Israel is God's _____ people.

4) The redemption of sinners:

We are slaves of sin. The price of our redemption is death. The one who pays that price for us is Jesus. Jesus is our

_____ .

In Mark 10:45 Jesus said he would give his life as a _____ for many.

Remember that the word **redeemed** means much the same as rescued or saved. When you think of salvation, think of redemption. We are in deep trouble and need to be saved — and salvation comes when the price is paid. This is redemption.

3. Look up Ephesians 2:1–10.

   a. According to v. 1, we are _____ in trespasses and sins.

   b. But God has made us _____

   with _____ . (v. 5)

   c. According to v. 4, why has God made us alive?

   _____

   d. In v. 8, it says God saved us by _____

   through _____ .

   e. **Grace** means favor that is not deserved. Do we deserve to be saved from sin? _____

   f. In v. 8, salvation or redemption is the _____ of God.

   g. According to v. 8 and 9, how much of our salvation do we work for? _____

4. Look up Ephesians 1:4–7.

   a. The words of these verses are addressed to Christians. According to v. 4, when did God choose us?

   _____

   b. Verse 4 says we were chosen that we should be

   _____ and _____

   before _____ .

   c. In v. 5 the word **predestined** means to plan. God planned (his decree) to rescue many, many sinners and adopt us through _____

   _____ .

   d. Verse 7 says that our redemption price is Jesus'

   _____ .

   This means he died and we can be freed from slavery to sin.

5. God chooses to save people.

Think about it

Thus the Bible teaches that even *before* he created the world, God chose to redeem many from sin. Those who are God's chosen ones are also called his elect. Jesus came to be the Redeemer of God's elect; his blood was the ransom to free them. God did not have to do this; he would have *been* right to receive the payment for our own sin through our death instead of sending Jesus to die for us.

a. Those who are God's chosen ones are also called his

_____ .

b. Who is the only Redeemer of God's elect? (S.C. #21)

_____

Think about it

Many people do not like this teaching that God has chosen some to be saved. Some do not like it because they are unbelievers and think they can live without God and do not like to be told they cannot. Others think that God is not being fair to choose some, since others who want to be saved could not come. And others think that if God has planned it all, then that does not really give man a choice.

As we studied in the lesson about revelation, there are many things about God and his ways that we cannot understand. But do not forget that God's wisdom is infinite, eternal, and unchangeable. That means he is able to have a plan that includes the choices of people.

Look up II Thessalonians 2:13.

Paul said *"But we ought always to give thanks to God for you, brothers beloved by the Lord, because God _____ you as the firstfruits to be _____, through sanctification by the Spirit and _____ in the truth."*

6. Review this lesson, then try to rewrite the answer to S.C. #20 in your own words. _____

_____

_____

_____

_____

_____

What do YOU think?

Date Completed _____

Parent's Initials_____

Lesson 9

Jesus Christ—His Person and Work

So far you have studied something of what God is like and what he has done. You have also learned about sin and how terrible it is and how God has planned to save people from their sin. This is **redemption**. But there can be no redemption without a **Redeemer**.

1. *Who is the Redeemer of God's elect?* (S.C. #21)

    _____ _____, *who, being*

    the eternal _____ *of* _____, *became*

    _____, *and so* _____, *and continueth to be,*

    _____ *and* _____ *in two distinct*

    _____, *and* _____ _____, *for ever.*

    This important answer has several parts:

    a. How many redeemers, or saviors from sin, are there? ___

        1) According to John 14:6, Jesus said no one could come to the Father except through _____ .

        2) In Acts 4:12, Peter said about Jesus, *"There is no other* _____ *under heaven given among men by which we must be saved."*

        3) In I Timothy 2:5, Paul said the only _____

           between God and men is the man _____

           _____ .

    b. S.C. #21 also says that Jesus, who was already the eternal _____ , became _____ . But when the Son of God, or God the Son, became man, he did not stop being God but even now continues to be both, in _____ distinct natures. Jesus has a divine nature and a human nature. He is not half man and half God, but **both** God and man.

1) Look up Matthew 1:18–25.

    a) According to vs. 18 and 20, the child Mary was expecting was from

    _____.

    b) The prophet the angel quoted in v. 23 was Isaiah.

    Look up Isaiah 7:14.

        i) What does Isaiah 7:14 say the virgin's child would be named?

        _____

        ii) What does Matthew 1:23 say that name means?

        _____

        iii) List the titles given to this child in Isaiah 9:6.

        _____

        _____

        _____

        _____

    So even Jesus' birth clearly teaches us that he is one person in two distinct natures.

2) Look up these verses from Jesus' life and tell whether they talk of his human or divine nature:

Matthew 8:1–3 _____

Matthew 12:46 _____

Matthew 8:24 _____

Matthew 14:18–21 _____

Matthew 8:26, 27 _____

Matthew 27:50 _____

3) Both of Jesus' natures are important for us. As **God**, Jesus is able to forgive our sin and give us a home in heaven. In Hebrews 12:2, Jesus is the _____ and _____ of our faith. As **man**, Jesus understood and experienced everything we

have, except _____. (Hebrews 4:15; S.C. #22) Jesus lived as Adam could have lived if he had not sinned; and when Jesus saves us, he wants us to live that way.

What do YOU think?

2. Jesus was a wonderful person and did many wonderful things. He showed us how important it is to be concerned for the poor and the sick. But what has caused poverty and sickness and death and hatred? _____

Because of this, Jesus had one main reason for coming, which was announced before he was born.

a. According to Matthew 1:21, why was he to be given the name Jesus? _____

_____

b. As our Redeemer, Jesus paid our ransom. According to Mark 10:45, what did he give as a ransom?

_____

c. The first four books of the New Testament tell of Jesus' life and death. These are not the four Gospels, as is often said, but it is the Gospel according to four different people. Who are these four?

_____ _____

_____ _____

d. The word Gospel means good news. And telling about Jesus' coming to save us is good news.

1) Look up I Corinthians 15:3, 4 and list the three facts about Jesus that were part of the Gospel Paul told them.

_____

_____

_____

2) How do you think it could be good news that someone as wonderful as Jesus died? Isn't it bad news? _____

_____

_____

e. Jesus' resurrection.

Think about it

The death of Jesus on the cross was extremely important. It was a death unlike any other death . For one thing, it was a death followed by resurrection. Jesus came from the tomb in a new kind of body — one that would never die. Jesus proved he was the Son of God who could take away our sin by rising from the dead.

Look up I Corinthians 15.

1) Read vs. 3–8. Do you think Paul (the writer) believed that Jesus rose from the dead? _____

How many times does Paul mention Jesus appeared after the resurrection? _____

2) According to v. 12, did some people in those days deny the idea of a resurrection? _____

3) According to v. 17, what is true if Christ was not raised? _____

_____

4) In v. 20 what is the fact about Christ? _____

_____

5) According to v. 22, Adam brought _____

and Christ brought _____ .

3. Look up S.C. #23. The three offices Christ our Redeemer executes for us are

_____

_____

_____

a. Prophet, priest, and king

A prophet takes a message from God and gives it to the people. A priest does the opposite; he goes from the people to God. Sinful people cannot go directly to a holy God, so the priest is the mediator or intercessor for the people.

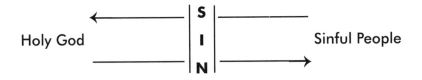

Holy God   **S I N**   Sinful People

In this diagram man is separated from God because of sin. One arrow represents the work of a prophet and one a priest. <u>Label the arrows correctly</u>.

Now briefly define the work of a king. _____

_____

_____

b. In the Old Testament these three offices were very important, but, with a few exceptions, were always held by different men. Can you think of an Old Testament prophet? _____

a priest? _____

a king? _____

What do YOU think?

c. Jesus carried out all three of these offices at the same time. Look up these verses and tell which of Jesus' three offices they describe.

Matthew 7:28, 29 _____

Hebrews 9:24–26 _____

Luke 4:16–21 _____

Hebrews 10:12–14 _____

I Corinthians 15:25 _____

Revelation 19:16 _____

Don't forget!

Date Completed _____

Parent's Initials_____

JESUS CHRIST– JUSTIFICATION AND ADOPTION

1. In lesson #9 we considered the three offices that Christ carries out as our Redeemer. What are they? (S.C. #23)

_____

This study will concentrate on one of those offices — Jesus our **Priest**. A **priest** is one who stands between God and the people. A priest is needed because God is holy and cannot meet with people who are sinful. So the people come to the priest, and the priest then goes to God.

a. What does a priest do? _____

_____

_____

b. God is _____, and people are _____.

Because God is holy ("infinite, eternal, and unchangeable, in his . . . <u>holiness</u>"), he is also just ("infinite, eternal, and unchangeable, in his . . . <u>justice</u>"). This means that when we break God's law (sin), God cannot simply forget what we do any more than a judge can forget that a man has committed a crime. The penalty for breaking God's law must be paid. That penalty, as we have seen, is death.

Think about it

2. Sin has a penalty.

 a. If a man robbed a bank and killed a guard in escaping, should he be punished according to the law?

 _____

 1) Would this mean the judge of the court where the man was tried did not like him? _____

 2) Suppose the bank robber was poor, should he still be punished? _____

 3) Suppose the man was sorry? _____

 b. God is our judge and his justice is perfect.

 1) Can he love us and be our judge at the same time?

 _____

 2) Is it unfair for God to judge us for our sin? _____

 _____

 3) What is the penalty for breaking God's law?

 _____

3. God is loving and just.

Think about it

In the Old Testament is a wonderful teaching about God's holiness and justice. God taught that, while he hated sin and could not forget it, he would allow a substitute to pay the penalty for sin. Animals (usually sheep or goats, or if you were poor, birds) could be brought to the priest as a sacrifice. The person bringing the animal confessed his sin and then killed the animal sacrifice. The penalty for sin is death — but death came to the animal instead of the person. The priest then caught some of the animal's blood and took it into the temple to show God that the penalty was paid. Then the person was forgiven his sin.

a. In the Old Testament, God taught that he would allow a
_____ to pay the penalty for sin.

b. What were these substitutes? _____

c. What did the blood show? _____

_____

d. Who took the blood in to God? _____

e. Because a substitute paid the penalty, the person's sins
were _____ .

f. Look up Leviticus 17:11.

1) What was the life of the flesh? _____

2) Blood was put on the altar to make atonement (pay
the penalty) for _____ .

g. According to Leviticus 22:21, the animal sacrifice had to
be _____ to be accepted.

4. So to be forgiven our sin we need two things — a **priest**
to go to God for us, and a **sacrifice of blood** to show the
penalty has been paid. Look up Hebrews 9.

a. What two things are necessary for God to forgive our
sin? _____

_____

b. According to Hebrews 9:11, who is our priest?

_____

c. According to 9:12, whose blood did he offer as a
sacrifice? _____

d. So who is both our priest and our sacrifice?

_____

e. According to 9:14, was Jesus the perfect ("*without blem-
ish*") sacrifice that was needed? _____

f. According to 9:14, what happens to our conscience because of Jesus' sacrifice? _____

_____

g. According to 9:25,26, how many times did Jesus need
to offer himself as a sacrifice? _____

h. Do you think Jesus' death was a great enough sacrifice
to pay the penalty for all our sin? _____

i. The Bible teaches that Jesus was our sacrifice once, but he is alive and continues to be our priest. Look up Hebrews 4:14–16. What does v. 16 say we should do because Jesus is our priest? _____

_____

5. Justification by faith

Think about it

So Jesus' death made possible something wonderful — our justification. The sin that puts a wall between man and God is taken away. The judge has administered justice, and we will never have to answer for our sin. Jesus has taken care of it. God not only forgives all our sin, but he also sees us as though we were as righteous as Jesus. Jesus' righteousness is like a beautiful coat that covers all our dirty clothes (our sin). The word used in the Bible for this is justification. People have tried to earn justification by doing good works, or giving money to the church, or following certain rules. But the Bible teaches that justification is God's gift. We only have to believe God when he promises to justify us because of Jesus. This is what the Bible means by "justification by faith."

a. What is justification? (S.C. #33) An act of God's free

_____, wherein he pardoneth _____ ,

and accepteth us as _____ in his

_____ , only for the _____

of _____ , _____ to

_____ , and received by _____ alone.

b. The catechism says that God "accepteth us as righteous." So when we believe in Jesus and God looks at us, whose righteousness does he see covering us like a beautiful coat? _____

c. How have people tried to earn justification? _____

_____

_____

d. Galatians 2:16 says a person is not justified by _____

_____

but through _____ in Jesus Christ.

e. According to Romans 5:1, what do we have because we are justified by faith? _____

_____

f. Why do you think so many people will not believe or accept God's promise to justify them through Jesus?

_____

_____

Do you believe that promise for yourself? _____

6. Adoption

The Bible teaches that when God forgives all of our sin and covers us with the righteousness of Christ because we trust Jesus (justification), something else very wonderful happens — we are adopted into God's family. We are made children of God by <u>adoption</u>.

Think about it

a. Think of someone you know who has been adopted (perhaps you have).

1) Does an adopted child take the name of the family? _____

What do YOU think?

2) Does an adopted child have all the privileges of a family member? _____

3) Is an adopted child a full member of the family?

_____

b. Adoption in God's family is the same. Look up Romans 8:15–17.

1) We did not receive the spirit of slavery to

_____ back into _____, but the

Spirit of _____, by whom we cry,

_____ _____ . (v. 15)

2) It is the Holy Spirit himself who bears witness with our spirits that we are _____ .
(v. 16)

3) Because we are children, we have an inheritance coming (we are heirs). Who will we share that inheritance with? (our fellow heir) _____ (v. 17)

c. What is adoption? (S.C. #34) "Adoption is an act of

God's _____, whereby we are _____

into the _____, and have a _____

to all the _____ of the _____

of _____."

Date Completed _____

Parent's Initials _____

Lesson 11

THE HOLY SPIRIT AND EFFECTUAL CALLING

In Lesson #10, the question was asked why so many do not want God's gift of justification. The answer goes back to the fact that we are sinners and do not really want God's way, even when it helps us. But God is so wonderful that he still loves us. God loves us so much that not only did the Son of God die for us, but the Spirit of God comes to us to show us we are sinners so that we will believe God's promise and be justified.

1. The Holy Spirit is God, the third person of the Holy Trinity. He is infinite, eternal, unchangeable in his Being and is to be worshipped along with the Father and the Son. Because he is spirit and invisible, we know the Holy Spirit by what he **does** more than by what he **is**. Look up the Gospel according to John.

    a. In John 1:33, John the Baptist said he baptized with _____ , but Jesus (on whom the Spirit descended) would baptize with the _____ .

    b. In v. 3:5, Jesus taught that a person must be born of water and the _____ to enter the kingdom of God. In 3:8 he said the Spirit is like the _____.

    c. In vs. 7:38,39, what did Jesus mean by rivers of living water coming from their hearts? _____

    _____

    Who would receive the Spirit? _____

    _____

    d. Even though the Holy Spirit had always been present, Jesus taught that he would give them the Spirit to live in them in a special way as he had not before. Just before he was crucified, Jesus taught us much about the Holy Spirit.

    1) In John 14:16, what is the Spirit called? _____

    _____

In 14:17 he is the Spirit of _____, whom the world could not receive because it did not _____ him or _____ him.

In 14:26 what will the Spirit do? _____

_____

_____

2) What will he do according to these verses:

15:26 _____

16:8 _____

16:13 _____

16:14 _____

2. One of the most important things the Holy Spirit does is to cause those who are dead in sin to be saved.

a. How do we take part in the redemption Christ bought? (S.C. #29) By the effectual _____

of it to us by his _____ .

Something that is **effectual** means that it works the way it is supposed to. Redemption works for us because the Holy Spirit is powerful enough to make it work.

b. How does the Holy Spirit work to apply redemption to us? (S.C. #30) By working _____

in us, and thereby uniting us to _____

in our _____ .

What does *effectual* mean? _____

_____

c. *What is effectual calling?* (S.C. #31) *It is the work of*

_____

1) *convincing us of* _____

_____

2) *enlightening our* _____

_____

3) *and renewing our* _____

_____ .

This is how he persuades and makes us able to embrace _____ freely offered to us in the Gospel.

d. In effectual calling, the Holy Spirit makes us see how much we need Christ. He makes us want to believe in Jesus, and then He gives us the faith we need. Do you think anyone would want to believe in Jesus without the effectual calling of the Spirit? _____

e. Look up I Corinthians 1:22–24. When Paul preached about Jesus' dying for them on the cross (*"Christ crucified"*), what was that preaching to the Jews? _____

_____

To the Gentiles (Greeks)? _____

But what was it to those whom the Holy Spirit was

calling? _____

_____

f. People respond differently to the gospel.

Imagine three people who sit near each other in a church. <u>Jim</u> is very smart and has read many books, <u>Joy</u> loves sports and doesn't like to sit still, and <u>Susan</u> is very good at music and wants to play in an orchestra. In church the speaker explains very carefully why Jesus died for them and how they can have him in their lives. Then he asks everyone who would like to believe in Christ to stay after church to talk some more about it. <u>Jim</u> goes out thinking that the talk was very boring. <u>Joy</u> jumps up to go play a game, glad the service is over, but <u>Susan</u> stays to talk to the speaker because she feels inside that having Jesus is more important than anything in the world.

Think about it

Think about what you have learned about effectual calling and I Corinthians 1:22–24 and explain why Susan believed in Jesus while Jim and Joy weren't ready to.

_____

_____

_____

_____

_____

_____

_____

_____

Date Completed _____

Parent's Initials_____

THE HOLY SPIRIT– REGENERATION AND CONVERSION

We are studying how the Holy Spirit applies to us the re-demption purchased by Christ. In Lesson #11 we learned that he begins through the work of effectual calling. Look at S.C. #31. By showing us our sin, making us understand who Jesus is, and causing us to want to believe in Jesus, what does the Holy Spirit persuade and enable us to do? _____

The Holy Spirit's working in us this way causes our **regeneration**. Look at that word. **Generate** means to *give life*, and **re** means *again*. So **regenerate** means to *give life again*. When the Holy Spirit regenerates us, we come from death (caused by sin) to life.

1. Define regeneration. _____

2. Look up John 3 where Jesus discusses regeneration. Regen-eration is another word for being **born again**.

    a. A man who was a very important religious leader came to Jesus at night. His name was (v. 1)

        _____ .

    b. Because it was not enough to be religious, Jesus said to him, *"Unless one is* _____ *he cannot see the kingdom of God."* (v. 3)

        Later in v. 7 he said, *"Do not marvel that I said to you, you must be* _____ *."*

    c. In explaining what he meant, Jesus said he had to be born of _____ and of the _____ . (v. 5)

        1) Water probably meant baptism by John the Baptist in repentance for sin. It could also refer to human birth.

2) But even repenting of sin is not enough; we must be changed by the Holy Spirit — born of the **Spirit**.

3. Look up John 1:12, 13. Who did God make his children?

Those who _____ Jesus and who were

born _____ .

4. Conversion

Think about it

Because the Holy Spirit calls and regenerates us, we are now able and willing to "embrace Jesus Christ freely offered to us in the Gospel." This decision to follow Jesus is called <u>conversion</u>. Conversion has two parts — faith and repentance. Faith means turning <u>to</u> Jesus to be our Master and Savior, and repentance means turning <u>from</u> our sin.

a. What are the two parts of conversion?

_____ and _____

1) Define faith: _____ to _____

2) Define repentance: _____ from _____

3) Notice the word "turning" is in both definitions.

a) Can there be true faith without repentance?

_____

Explain. _____

_____

b) Can there be true repentance if there is no faith? _____

Explain. _____

_____

b. Look up S.C. #85. What does God require of us, that we may escape his wrath and curse due to us for sin?

1) _____ in Jesus Christ

2) _____ unto life

3) diligent use of all the _____

_____

_____

(We will study these later.)

c. What is faith in Jesus Christ? (S.C. #86) A saving grace, whereby we _____ and _____ upon him_____ for _____,

as he is offered to us in the _____ .

1) Is it true faith just to know that he is God and that he died on the cross for us? _____

2) True faith means we **rest** (put all our weight) on Jesus — he is our only hope for salvation. **Write down** one example from everyday life of how we put complete faith in something to support us.

_____

_____

_____

What do you think?

d. What is repentance unto life? (S.C. #87) A saving grace, whereby a sinner, out of a true sense of _____ ,

and apprehension of the _____ of God in Christ, _____

his sin, _____ from it unto _____,

with full purpose of, and endeavor after, _____

_____ .

1) Is it enough to be sorry for sin without turning away from it? _____

2) Can a person be **sure** of God's forgiveness through Christ if he truly repents? _____

3) How do you think a person can be sure he is truly repenting? _____

_____

61

5. Different people have different experiences.

Think about it

> People often have very exciting conversions (like the Apostle Paul) and can remember exactly when and how they were converted. Other people truly believe in Jesus and follow him but do not remember just when they were converted. What is important for all people is that they <u>follow</u> Jesus and trust only in him for salvation. If they are, they can say they have been converted.

a. Suppose you have a friend in whom the Holy Spirit is working. He really wants to pray to God, to repent and believe in Jesus, and be saved. He asks you to write a prayer that would say the right things to God so he could become a child of God. **Write out** the prayer you would give your friend to pray. _____

_____

_____

_____

_____

What do YOU think?

b. Have you been converted to Jesus Christ? Explain your answer. If you want to be but aren't sure how, write down your questions. It is important to answer this carefully. _

_____

_____

_____

Date Completed _____

Parent's Initials_____

THE HOLY SPIRIT—SANCTIFICATION AND ASSURANCE

We have been studying the work of the Holy Spirit as he applies the redemption bought by Christ. First he **effectually calls** and **regenerates** us (*"born of the Spirit"*). But just as a new baby grows up, so the Holy Spirit causes the one born again to grow up. This is called **sanctification**.

1. List the three things the Holy Spirit does to apply redemption to us.

    _____

    _____

    _____

2. According to S.C. #32, what are the three benefits that come in this life to those who are effectually called? They

    partake of _____, _____,

    and _____ and the several benefits which

    flow from them.

3. Look up S.C. #35.

    a. Notice that S.C. #33 says justification is an **act** of God's free grace, #34 says adoption is an **act** of God's free grace, but #35 says sanctification is the _____ of God's free grace. When we are justified (forgiven all our sin and clothed in the righteousness of Christ) and adopted (taken into God's family), those happen once and will never change. But sanctification will go on until we go to be with Jesus. The change made by regeneration will always affect us.

b. According to S.C. #35, what two things happen to us when the Holy Spirit sanctifies us? We are renewed in the whole man after the _____ , and are _____ to

_____

and _____ .

1) *"We are renewed in the whole man"* because the Holy Spirit has killed our old sinful nature and has put a new nature in us.

a) Who were first *"after the image of God"*?

_____ and _____

b) But Adam and Eve lost their innocent nature. Who next had a perfect and sinless nature?

_____

c) So the Holy Spirit is at work making us like Jesus. He took away the Adam (old) nature (dead in sin) and is making us more and more like Jesus.

d) Look up Romans 6 — an important chapter about sanctification.

i) According to v. 5, if we have been united to Christ in his _____, we will also be united with him in his _____. If this is true, what does v. 6 say happened to the old self (old man, old nature)?_____

_____.

ii) What does v. 7 say is true because the old nature has died? _____

_____

iii) According to v. 8, what do we believe happens since we have died (the old self crucified) with Christ? _____

_____

iv) That living with Christ means **now**, not in the future. Verse 11 says we must consider (believe) ourselves _____ to sin and _____ to God in Christ Jesus.

what do
YOU think?

64

Just as we believe the Gospel _about Jesus_ — that he died and rose again from the dead — we are taught here that the most important part of sanctification is believing the Gospel _about ourselves_ that we have _died_ with him and have been _raised_ with him. Often we do not feel alive in Christ, but we still need to believe what the Gospel teaches about being united to Christ.

Think about it

v. But even when we believe the Gospel we still sin. Romans 6:12 says, _"Let not sin therefore reign in your _____

_____."_ v. 13 says not to present

your _____

to sin because you have been brought

from _____ to _____.

So even though we sin, sin will have no

_____ over us (v. 14) since

we are not under _____ but under

_____.

This can be very confusing. Try to **explain** how a Christian can be changed on the inside by the Holy Spirit and yet still sin.

_____

_____

_____

_____

_____

_____

What do YOU think?

2) S.C. #35 says the Spirit enables us more and more to die unto sin (the old nature has less and less power over us) and more and more to live unto righteousness (becoming like Christ).

   a) Even though the Spirit is working in us, he is not forcing us. What does Ephesians 4:30 warn us not to do? _____

   b) We must cooperate with the Spirit as he works in us. What do these verses tell us to do?

   Ephesians 4:22 _____the old self

   Ephesians 4:24 _____ the new self

   Ephesians 4:27 _____

   no _____ to the devil

   Ephesians 4:32 _____ to one another,

   _____, _____ one another

   Ephesians 5:2 _____ in love

   Ephesians 5:11 _____

   the unfruitful works of darkness.

   Ephesians 5:18 _____ with the Spirit

3) According to S.C. #36, what are the five benefits which accompany our justification, adoption, and sanctification? _____

   _____

   _____

4. Assurance

Think about it

Notice especially the benefit called "assurance of God's love." The Bible teaches that a person who is truly born of God (regeneration) can be certain that he or she belongs to God. And that no matter what happens in the future, God will always hold on to his chosen child. This is called <u>assurance of salvation.</u>

a) Define assurance. _____

_____

_____

b) Look up Romans 8:38, 39. Paul had assurance. What did he believe could separate him from the love of God in Christ? _____

c) Look up I John (not the Gospel of John). This book of the Bible was written to help Christians have assurance. Look up these verses and tell how we can know we are born of God and have eternal life.

2:3: We know that we have come to **know** him if

_____ .

3:14: We **know** that we have passed out of death into life because _____

_____ .

4:13: We **know** that we abide in him and he is in us because _____

_____

4:15: Whoever confesses that _____

_____

_____God abides in him and he in God.

5:18: We **know** that everyone who has been born of God _____

_____

(that means does not "keep on sinning all the time").

d) Do you have assurance that you are saved? Explain your answer._____

_____

_____

_____

What do YOU think?

Date Completed _____

Parent's Initials_____

THE FUTURE

The past several lessons have been studies of how the Holy Spirit applies the redemption bought by Christ. This lesson is a study of the final stage of redemption called <u>glorification</u>. Glorification means finally becoming what God saved us to become — perfect sons and daughters of God. Glorification will happen only when Jesus comes back.

1.   Define glorification. _____

_____

a.   When will it happen? _____

_____

b.   Look up Romans 8:29,30. Those whom he foreknew

he predestined to _____

_____that he (Jesus) might be

_____.

And those whom he _____ , he also

_____ ; those he called, he also

_____ ; those he justified, he

also _____ .

So glorification is just as much part of salvation as calling or justification. God saved us to become just like Jesus, and that will happen.

2. But before Jesus returns, many people will die.

    a. Look up S.C. #37. The _____ of believers
       are at their death made perfect in _____ , and
       do _____ pass into _____ ; and their
       _____ , being still united to Christ, do rest in
       their _____ till the _____ .

    b. This answer says that before the resurrection, the **souls** of
       believers go to be with Jesus, but the **bodies** are buried.
       Look up Philippians 1:21–23. The Apostle Paul thought
       he might die soon.

       1) In v. 21 what did he say death would be?

          _____

       2) In v. 23, if he departed (died), where would he
          be? _____

       3) Why was Paul not afraid to die? _____

          _____

3. Jesus taught us to expect him to return to the earth. Many
   people have tried to figure out when and have been wrong.
   Jesus warned us not to do that, but he did tell us to be ready
   always.

    a. Look up Acts 1:9–11. This happened 40 days after the
       resurrection of Jesus.

       1) According to v. 9, what happened to Jesus?

          _____

       2) What did the angels promise in v. 11? _____

          _____

    b. Look up I Thessalonians 5:2–5.

       1) According to v. 2, what will Jesus' coming be like?

          _____

       2) But, according to v. 4, should a Christian be surprised
          by Jesus' return? _____

          Most people will be surprised, but this seems to
          say somehow Christians will be aware of what is
          happening.

We are to live every day expecting Jesus to return. But the Bible does not give precise details about everything that will happen when he does. Some people are sure Jesus will reign as King over the earth. Others think the idea of his reign is a symbol for his Kingship. We must respect such differences as long as they are honest attempts to interpret the Bible. But the Bible is clear about certain amazing events that will happen.

Think about it

a. **The resurrection**. Look up I Thessalonians 4:16,17.

1) In v. 16 what three sounds announce Jesus' coming down? _____

_____

_____

2) In v. 16 what happens to the dead in Christ?

_____

3) Then in v. 17 what happens to the Christians who are still alive? _____

_____

4) Where will all Christians be forever? (v. 17)

_____

So when Jesus returns, he will remake dead bodies so that they will be like his resurrection body. He was resurrected after three days. Resurrection for most Christians will not come so quickly.

b. **Destruction and remaking the earth**. Sin has affected the rest of God's creation, and when Jesus returns, all the scars of sin will be taken away. Look up II Peter 3:8–13.

1) According to v. 10, what will happen to the heavens? _____

And the heavenly bodies? _____

And the earth? _____

2) Why does v. 13 say this should not upset us?

_____

_____

3) How should this influence our daily living? (v. 11)

_____

c. **The end of Satan and all Jesus' enemies**. Look up I Corinthians 15:20–26.

1) What are the two resurrections mentioned in v. 21–23? _____

_____

2) In the end (v. 24), Jesus will deliver the _____

to God the Father after _____

everything that is against God.

3) According to v. 26, what is the final enemy to be destroyed? _____

Man brought death because of sin; Jesus will one day come to destroy death forever.

d. **Final judgment**. Look up Revelation 20:11–15.

1) What kind of throne is in v. 11? _____

_____

2) In v. 12 after the books were opened (probably listing what everyone had done), a second book was opened. What was it? _____

3) According to vs. 12–13, who will be before the judgment throne? _____

And how are they judged? _____

_____

4) What is the second death? (v. 14) _____

_____

5) Who was sent away from God? (v. 15) _____

_____

What do you think the Book of Life is? _____

_____

_____

6) According to S.C. #38, believers being _____

in glory, shall be openly _____

and _____

in the day of judgment.

This means if we belong to Jesus when we stand before God at the judgment, we will not be condemned.
Jesus took our judgment on the cross.

e. **Heaven**. After the judgment all believers will be like Jesus
completely, and we shall live forever with God.

1) What is the second thing S.C. #38 says will happen to believers at the resurrection when they
are raised up in glory? They will be "*made _____*

_____

in the _____

of _____ *to all eternity.*"

2) Look up Revelation 22:1–5. This is a picture of
heaven.

a) Where does the idea of the "*tree of life*" (v. 2) come
from? (Genesis 2:9; 3:22,23)

_____

b) There is no longer any _____ . (v. 3)

c) They will see his _____ . (v. 4)

Date Completed _____

Parent's Initials_____

THE CHURCH–JOINING THE VISIBLE CHURCH

We have been studying about our great God and his wonderful plan for redeeming people dead in sin and bringing them finally to glorification. But there is one more part of this plan that we need to study carefully. It is God's plan that while they live on earth his people gather together and form what Jesus called his <u>Church</u>. When people are truly born of God, they automatically become part of the one great Church of Jesus. Sometimes this is called the <u>invisible</u> church because only God knows exactly who its members are. The whole invisible church will be together when Jesus returns. Usually when the word <u>church</u> is used, it refers to an actual gathering of God's people somewhere on earth. This is sometimes called the <u>visible</u> church. In Lesson I you learned that God had always had a visible church, even though the organization of it had changed. At first it was a family (Abraham), then a nation (Israel). Since the coming of Jesus, the visible church has been formed by groups of people from all nations, brought together by the Holy Spirit.

1. Fill in the blanks with either **invisible** or **visible**:

   All people of every age who have been or will be born
   of God are made part of the _____
   church. The _____ church will be complete
   when Jesus returns. Usually when we read or think
   about the church it means a gathering of people here
   on earth, the _____ church. This
   _____ church is never perfect. It can happen that those who are never born of God join the
   church as though it were just another organization. Our
   church, called _____ Church,
   is a _____ church.

Think about it

> To be saved, each person must decide to believe in Jesus and follow him. But while that is an individual choice, once you make that choice you become part of a <u>family</u>. If your parents had decided to believe in Jesus, then you are already in the family — but now it is time for you to say for yourself you want to be part of the family.
>
> The Bible also says you become part of a <u>body</u>. These are just two of the terms used to describe the Church.

2. Name two terms used to describe the Church.

   _____

   a. According to S.C. #34, how did we become members of
      God's family? _____

      1) Who is the father in the family? _____

      2) Who is the oldest brother in the family? (He was not

What do you think?

adopted.) _____

3) Who are our brothers and sisters in this family?

_____

4) How many of the privileges of God's children do we have? (S.C. #34) _____

5) What responsibilities do you think we have to the Father? _____

_____

6) What responsibilities do you think we have to our brothers and sisters? _____

_____

b. Look up I Corinthians 12.

1) In v. 27 the whole church is called the _____

of Christ and each person is a _____ of that body.

2) Is every part of the body the same? (v. 14) _____

3) What five parts are mentioned in vs. 15–17?

_____

_____

4) What do you think is being taught about the church? _____

_____

_____

5) Who fits the parts of the body together to make it work? (v. 13) _____

6) Do you think you are an important part of the body of Christ? _____

Explain. _____

_____

_____

_____

What do
You think?

There's more …

c. The visible and invisible church

**Think
about it**

The visible church is different from the invisible church in at least three ways.

1)   The visible church needs to be <u>organized</u> with leaders and discipline. As a group of people who still are sinners, Christians need direction and sometimes correction. In heaven our sin will be completely gone, and Jesus will be there so we will not need the same kind of organization.

2)   The visible church was given <u>sacraments</u> to administer to remind us of Jesus. The sacraments are to help Christians grow in faith, but in heaven we will not need them because Jesus himself will be there.

3)   In the visible church, the most important unit is the <u>family</u>. God created the family, and he wants his church to make the family stronger. In heaven Jesus has told us that family life will be very different from what it is now.

3.   What are three important ways to understand the visible church?

a. It needs to be _____ .

b. It administers the _____ .

c. Its most important unit is the _____ .

4.   It is a very important part of your commitment to follow Jesus that you commit to be a member of his *visible* church. This is often called "joining the church." This is a very serious commitment, which is one reason we have taken this time to help you prepare to become a "communicant member" (we talked about this in lesson 1, p. 4).

When you join a visible church you meet with the elders and then stand before the church and the Lord to answer several questions. Now it is time to read these questions and make sure you can answer them sincerely.

Membership vows for our church:

(**Note**: Your teacher will give you a copy of the questions that your church uses when it receives communicant members.)

Do you feel you understand each one of them? _____

Write down what you do not understand. _____

_____

_____

Can you answer each one of them with "Yes"? _____

5. When you join a church you should expect to support the church in its life and ministry. You will help the church, and the church will help you grow stronger in Christ. Here are four ways you can support your church:

    a. **Worship**. Worship means giving God the Father, Son, and Holy Spirit the praise and honor that is due. We can and should worship alone, but we also must worship together. Study the worship service in your church bulletin and list several different ways God is worshipped. _____

_____

b. **Fellowship**. Although we are to love all persons, even our enemies, Jesus taught that we have a special relationship to other Christians. According to Acts 4:32, how did the company of believers feel about one another? _____

_____

c. **Giving**. One mark of true Christians is that just as Jesus gave to them, so they give to others. The standard from the beginning of the Bible is that ten percent of what we have should be given back to God. This is called a **tithe**. But look up Acts 4:34, 35. How much were those Christians willing to give? _____

_____

d. **Witnessing**. We have such good news about Jesus we need to tell others. According to Acts 4:33, what were the apostles doing? _____

_____

And what came upon them all? _____

Date Completed _____

Parent's Initials_____

THE CHURCH–
HOW IT WORKS

1. List the three things true about the working of the visible church mentioned in Lesson 15. (page 76, question 3)

    a. It needs to be _____ .

    b. It administers the _____ .

    c. Its basic unit is the _____ .

    Now we will study how the visible church should be organized. Different Christians have interpreted the Bible differently on this matter, and this is one reason for denominations. What follows is how Presbyterians and many others understand the church should be organized.

2. A new beginning for the church

When *Jesus* began his church, the church had a new beginning. Before, it had been a nation (Israel); but now anyone, Jew or Gentile, could join his church. He sent his apostles out in the power of the Holy Spirit to preach the Gospel and start churches. God gave the apostles new Christians who became leaders and started other churches. And from those churches came more leaders going out to preach and start more churches.

Think about it

    a. Whom did Jesus send out as leaders of the first churches? _____

1) Should the apostles be considered missionaries?

_____

2) What then do you think missionaries today should be trying to do? _____

_____

What do you think?

b. Look up Titus 1.

1) Who was the apostle sent by Jesus? (v. 1) _____

2) What leader did Paul send to start churches? (v. 4) _____

3) Why was Titus in Crete? (v. 5) _____

_____

_____

4) The leaders of churches are called (v. 5) _____ .

What is another name for elders according to v. 7? _____

5) What is one of the most important jobs of the elder/overseer according to v. 9? _____

_____

c. Look up I Timothy 3.

1) Read vs. 1–7 and describe briefly the qualifications for elder. _____

_____

_____

2) What is the second officer described in vs. 8–13?

_____

3) So the two main church officers are **elders** to lead spiritually and do the teaching and preaching and **deacons** who serve the people of the church and community. Many churches have a deacons fund to help the poor and others with special needs.

3. Presbyterians talk about ruling and teaching elders. Most churches have several **ruling elders**. The **teaching elder** has special gifts and training and does most of the teaching and preaching. He is often called the pastor or minister of a church.

What is the name of a ruling elder you know?

_____

What is the name of a teaching elder you know?

_____

a. The Session

The elders of the church meet frequently. When they do, the group of elders is called the _Session_. In its meetings, the Session meets with people who want to join the church. It plans for church activities, discusses and prays about members who have problems, and does many other things. If a member of the church is living in a way that the Bible clearly says is sinful, it is sometimes necessary for the Session to discipline that member. The first reason for discipline is to help the person to repent; but if he will not change, then he can no longer _be_ a member. Church discipline is very serious and is only done after much prayer.

Think about it

1) What are the elders of a church called? _____

2) What are some things the Session does when it meets? _____

_____

_____

3) Why is it sometimes necessary to discipline a member of the church? _____

_____

_____

b. The Presbytery

Think about it

Sometimes elders from several churches meet together to do things too big or too important for just one church to do, such as examining teaching elders. Since in the Greek language the word for elder is presbyter, the meeting of elders is called <u>Presbytery</u>. This is the beginning of the name <u>Presbyterian</u> — a church led by elders.

Explain why our church is called Presbyterian. _____

_____

_____

c. The General Assembly

Think about it

Sometimes several Presbyteries meet. This is called <u>General Assembly</u>. They meet to do work too big or too important for just one Presbytery. In Acts 15 there was a General Assembly when all the Christian leaders gathered to discuss an important question.

d. The groups mentioned above are often called the **courts** of the church. We have studied **three** courts of the church.

When elders of one church meet, it is the _____ .

When Sessions from several churches meet it is the

_____ .

When several Presbyteries meet it is the _____

_____ .

4.   Some church history

Presbyterians are part of a large family of churches known as the <u>Reformed</u> churches. The word Reformed comes from Reformation, a great time of revival in Europe from 1520–1570. The greatest leader of the Reformed churches was a scholar and Bible teacher named <u>John Calvin</u>. For this reason, Reformed churches are also called Calvinist churches. In 1643 Reformed leaders of England, Ireland, and Scotland — mostly Puritans and Presbyterians — met to write down an explanation of the teachings of the Bible. That explanation is called the <u>Westminster Confession of Faith</u>. Presbyterians still teach that this is the *best explanation of what the Bible teaches*. To help understand the Confession, the leaders who met at Westminster also wrote the Larger Catechism and the Shorter Catechism (which you have *been studying*).

Think about it

a.   Answer these questions from the above paragraph.

1)   Presbyterian churches are part of a large family of churches known as _____ churches.

2)   Reformed churches are sometimes called

_____churches after the great Bible

scholar _____ .

3)   English-speaking Calvinists met in 1643 and set forth the teachings of the Bible in a document known as the _____

Confession of _____ . They also wrote the

_____ and _____Catechisms.

83

b. Unfortunately many Presbyterians as well as others no longer believe in the Bible the way Christians have from the days of Jesus. It has even been necessary to start new churches so that people could be free from false teachers.

1) Why has it been necessary for some to leave their old churches and start new ones? _____

   _____

2) What is the name of your denomination? _____

   _____

What do YOU think?

Don't forget!

Date Completed _____

Parent's Initials _____

THE CHURCH— CHRISTIAN LIVING

As we have seen, the Church is very important because it is part of God's plan, not just a human organization. The Church is also important because it is where the Holy Spirit will help you grow as a Christian.

1. Look up S.C. #85 and #88.

    a. In S.C. #85, what three things does God require of us, that we may escape his wrath and curse?

    _____ in Jesus Christ, _____ unto

    life, with the diligent use of all the _____

    whereby Christ communicateth to us the benefits

    of redemption.

    b. Faith and repentance we have studied as the two parts
    of _____ .
    (Lesson #12, Question 4) Of course, we don't stop
    turning to Jesus, which is _____, or turning
    from our sin, which is _____, once
    we are converted. Both of them will grow because in
    sanctification we see more of our sin and more of our
    need for Jesus.

    c. The "outward means," also called **means of grace**.
    "Means" is an old word that describes things that help us
    experience God's grace. They are what God has given to
    help us grow in faith and repentance so we learn more
    and more about God's grace in our lives. S.C. #88 says
    we should concentrate "especially" on three of these
    means. These are _____ ,

    _____, and _____ .

    You cannot grow if you do not read and study the Bible
    (**the Word**); you cannot grow if you do not take part
    in the life of the church (**the sacraments**); you cannot
    grow if you do not spend time praying to God (**prayer**).
    Sometimes people remain baby Christians all of their

lives. Explain how this is possible. _____

_____

_____

    d. So S.C. #85 says we must have _____
use of all the outward means. Spiritual growth does not
happen accidentally or automatically.

2. What are the ways your church is helping you to study and
know the Word (the Bible)? _____

_____

_____

3. What are the ways your church is helping you learn to
pray? _____

_____

_____

4. Sacraments

Think about it

> Very important among the means of grace are the <u>Sacraments</u>. A sacrament can *be* defined as an outward symbol of a spiritual truth. Jesus gave us the sacraments we observe as a way to remember him as well as to grow in his grace. The sacraments themselves have no special power; they are only symbols, but when we receive them in faith we receive great blessings.

    a. Define a sacrament. _____

_____

    1) Who taught us to observe the sacraments we do?
(S.C. #92) _____

2) Which are the sacraments of the New Testament? (S.C. #93) _____

_____

3) Do the sacraments have any power in themselves? _____

4) What happens when we receive the sacraments by faith? _____

_____

b. Baptism

Baptism is a sacrament in which water is used to symbolize the washing away of our sin and our being united to Christ. Baptism is also an outward mark that shows who belongs to God's family in the New Testament church, just as circumcision did in the Old Testament.

Think about it

1) What two things does baptism symbolize?

_____

_____

2) In the Old Testament church, the outward mark of membership in God's family was circumcision. What is the mark of the New Testament church?

_____

3) According to Matthew 28:19, whose name should be used in baptism? _____

_____

There's more ...

4) Who should be baptized?

Think about it

There are two groups: 1) those who come to trust in Jesus and join the visible church, and 2) the children of those families already in the visible church. Some teach that only the first group should be baptized — that even children of Christian parents should wait until they confess faith in Jesus before being baptized. But this overlooks the important truth that the most important unit of the church is the family. In the Old Testament, children were to be circumcised; so in the New Testament, children are to be baptized. This is a testimony that the whole family belongs to the Lord and to his visible church.

a) What two groups of people should be baptized?

   i) _____

   _____

   ii) _____

   _____

b) When Christian parents have their children baptized, what does this show? _____

   _____

   _____

   i) Do those children still need to believe in Jesus when they are old enough to understand? _____

   ii) Does baptism mean that children will automatically believe? _____

iii) Should children be baptized whose parents have never trusted in Jesus and joined the church? _____

iv) Look up Acts 16:14, 15, 32, 33. What happened after the parents believed in Jesus? _____

5) How should we baptize?

Since the Holy Spirit was poured out on the believers, it could be that John baptized Jesus by pouring out water on him. Therefore, some baptize by pouring out water as a symbol of the Holy Spirit. Others baptize by sprinkling water as a symbol of cleansing. Still others immerse to show death and resurrection. Most Presbyterians pour or sprinkle. The Bible is not clear enough on how to baptize to insist that only one way is right.

Think about it

When John the Baptist baptized people, he said, "I baptize you with water for _____....

He will baptize you with _____

and with _____." (Matthew 3:11)

a) How do most Presbyterians baptize? _____

_____

b) Which is the right way? _____

_____

c. The **Lord's Supper**, also called **Communion**, is a sacrament which uses the symbols of bread and wine to remind us of Jesus' death. They teach us the Gospel and give us an opportunity to believe in Jesus (_____) and turn from our sin (_____). So this is a very important means of _____.

1) Look up I Corinthians 11.

   a) When did Jesus begin the Lord's Supper? (v. 23) _____

   b) What does the broken bread symbolize? (v. 24) _____

   c) What does the wine cup (juice of grapes) symbolize? (v. 25) _____

   d) When will we stop having the Lord's Supper? (v. 26) _____

   e) What should a person do before taking the Lord's Supper? (v. 28) _____

   f) What is true of those who are careless or make fun of the Lord's Supper? (v. 29) _____

     _____

   g) Do you think a person who has never trusted Jesus should take the Lord's Supper? _____

     Explain. _____

     _____

2) Look up I Corinthians 10:16. It says the cup of blessing is a _____ in the _____ of Christ, and the bread that we break is a _____ in the _____ of Christ.

3) If the bread and wine are only symbols, why do you think Communion services are so special and sacred for Christians? _____

   _____

   _____

5. A great deal more could be said about each of these things, and surely other means of grace could be listed. But to complete this series of studies, think again about what God has done for you. Then write out a prayer telling him what you want him to do with your life and your future. _____

_____

_____

_____

What do YOU think?